United States
Department of
Agriculture

Forest
Service

**North Central
Research Station**

**Resource Bulletin
NC-259**

Kansas' Forest Resources in 2004

W. Keith Moser, Mark H. Hansen, Gary J. Brand, and Melissa Powers

North Central Research Station
U.S. Department of Agriculture - Forest Service
1992 Folwell Avenue
Saint Paul, Minnesota 55108
2006
www.ncrs.fs.fed.us

CONTENTS

Kansas' Forest Resources in 2004

The North Central Research Station's Forest Inventory and Analysis (NCFIA) program began fieldwork for the fifth forest inventory of Kansas' forest resources in 2001. This inventory initiated the new annual inventory system in which one-fifth of the field plots (considered one panel) in the State are measured each year. A complete inventory consists of measuring, compiling, and reporting the data for all plots in all five panels. Once the plots in all panels have been measured, each will be remeasured approximately every 5 years. For example, the field plots measured in 2003 will be remeasured in 2008.

In 2004, NCFIA continued the annual inventory effort with the fourth panel of the fifth Kansas forest inventory. Previous inventories of Kansas are dated 1936, 1965, 1981, and 1994 (Kansas State College 1939, Chase and Strickler 1968, Spencer *et al.* 1984, Raile and Spencer 1984, Leatherberry *et al.* 1999). This fifth inventory of Kansas' forest resources will be completed in 2005. However, because each year is a systematic sample of the State's forest and timely information is needed about Kansas' forest resources, estimates have been prepared from data gathered during the first 4 years of the inventory. Measurements from four panels, approximately 80 percent of the field plots of the complete inventory, are the basis for the estimates presented in this report. The underlying data are a combination of measurements for the first year's panel in 2001, the second year's panel in 2002, the third year's panel in 2003, and the fourth year's panel in 2004. The results presented are estimates based on sampling techniques; estimates for this report were compiled assuming the 2001, 2002, 2003, and 2004 data represent one sample. As additional annual panels are completed, the precision of the estimates will increase and additional data will be released.

Estimates from new inventories are often compared with estimates from earlier inventories to determine trends in forest resources. However, for the comparisons to be valid, the procedures used in the two inventories must be similar. As a result of our ongoing efforts to improve the efficiency and reliability of the inventory, several changes in procedures and definitions have been made since the last Kansas inventory in 1994 (Leatherberry *et al.* 1999). Although these changes will have some impact on statewide estimates of forest area, timber volume, and tree biomass, they may have significant impacts on plot classification variables such as forest type and stand-size class. Some of these changes make it inappropriate to directly compare portions of the 2001-2004 estimates with those published for earlier inventories. Except for oak/hickory, forest type descriptions in this report are categorized by broad groups and species not necessarily found in Kansas. Forest type subcategories more accurately describe the forests of the State. These subcategories include elm/ash/locust for maple/beech/birch, eastern redcedar/hardwood for oak/pine, and eastern redcedar for pinyon/juniper.

RESULTS

Area

Forest land area was 2.13 million acres in 2004 (table 1). Five percent of forest land in Kansas is owned by public agencies and 94.7 percent is owned by private landowners. More than 5.5 percent of forest land area is dominated by conifers, and 93.4 percent is dominated by hardwoods, and the remainder is classified as nonstocked[1]. Oak/hickory forests constitute 56 percent of the total hardwood area. The

About the Authors:

W. Keith Moser, Mark H. Hansen, and Gary J. Brand are Research Foresters with the North Central Research Station, St. Paul, MN.

Melissa Powers is a Forest Resource Specialist with the Kansas Forest Service, Manhattan, KS.

---

[1]Nonstocked land is timberland less than 10 percent stocked with all live trees.

pinyon/juniper forest group (primarily eastern redcedar)[2] constituted 89.1 percent of all forest land dominated by conifers.

Forest land is defined as land 1 acre in size, 120 feet in width, and possessing 10 percent stocking of live trees. It has three components:

1. Timberland[3]—forest land not restricted from harvesting by statute, administrative regulation, or designation and capable of growing trees at a rate of 20 cubic feet per acre per year

2. Reserved forest land—land restricted from harvesting by statute, administrative regulation, or designation (e.g., national parks and lakeshores, Federal wilderness areas)

3. Other forest land—land not capable of growing trees at a rate of 20 cubic feet per acre per year and not restricted from harvesting

_____

[2] In inventories before 1999, eastern redcedar was distinguished from pinyon/juniper.

[3] Timberland may not be equivalent to the area actually available for commercial timber harvesting or other access. The actual availability of land for various uses depends upon owner decisions that consider economic, environmental, and social factors.

Timberland area, 2.05 million acres, has continued to increase since its low point in the 1936 inventory (fig. 1). The significant jump in forest land and timberland area since the last periodic inventory is due to many factors, including the conversion of croplands and pastures to forest, the growth of trees on poorly stocked lands, and a definitional change. Previously, most of the forest lands that were grazed or that provided shelter from the wind were not classified as forest land. Since 2001, such lands have been classified as forest land if they meet the forest land definition.

The hardwood forest types dominate the timberland area (table 2), particularly the oak/hickory group (table 3, fig. 2). Hardwoods made up 93.4 percent of the total acreage, 88.3 percent of all public land acreage, and 93.7 percent of all private landholdings. Most forest type groups, except for the pinyon/juniper (eastern redcedar) group, are in the sawtimber or poletimber stand-size classes.

Figure 3 shows the area of timberland by stand-size class over the years. The areas in poletimber and sawtimber classes have steadily increased since the 1965 inventory.

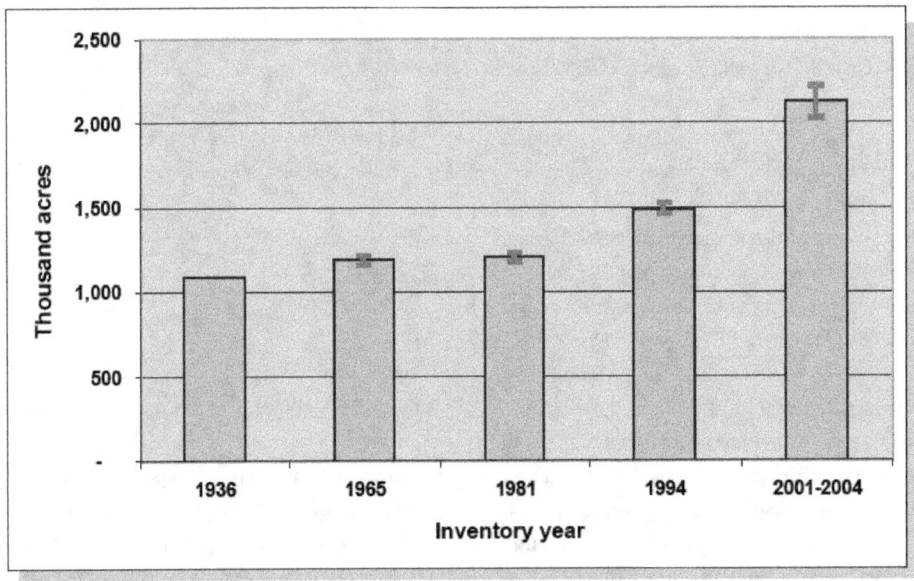

Figure 1. — *Area of timberland, Kansas, 1936-2004. (Note: The sampling error associated with an inventory estimate is represented by the vertical line at the top of its bar. No sampling error was available for the 1936 survey; timberland area was calculated using the total forest land area for 1936 multiplied by a ratio of timberland to total forest land from 1965.)*

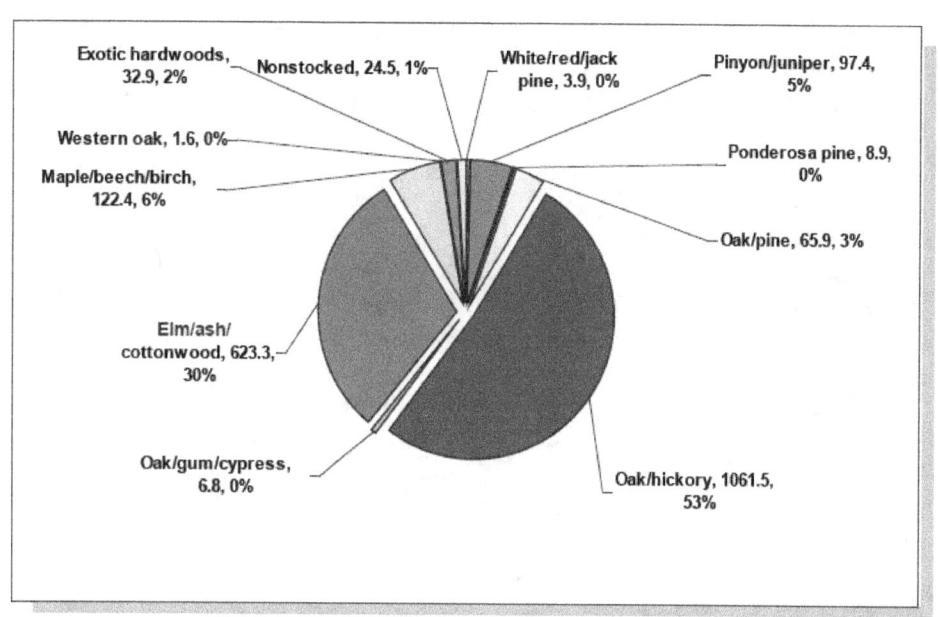

Figure 2. — *Area of timberland by forest type group[1], in thousands of acres, for Kansas, 2001-2004.*

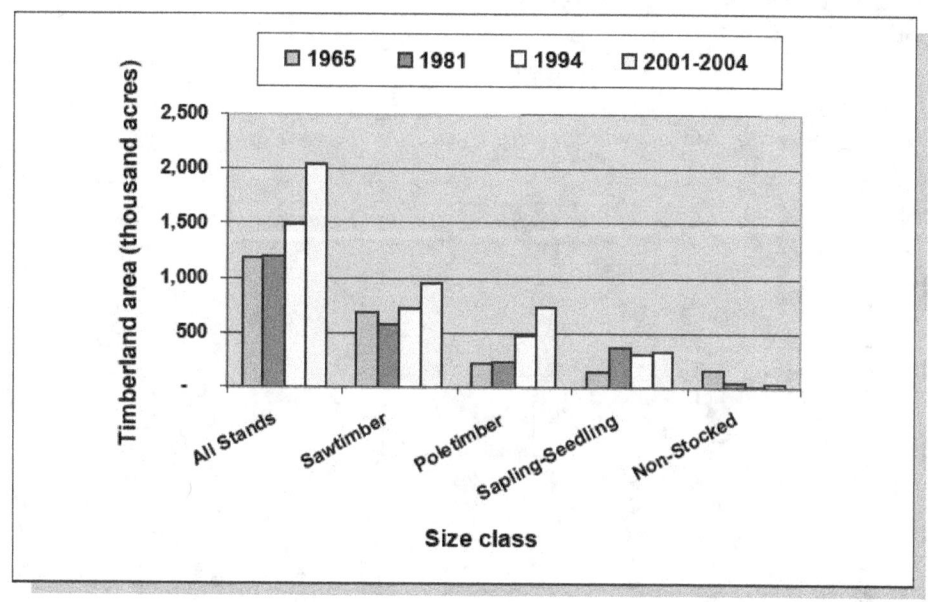

Figure 3. — *Area of timberland by stand-size class, Kansas, 1965-2004[2].*

---

[1]Under Forest Inventory and Analysis classifications, forest type groups are composed of several, sometimes related, forest types. For example, the oak/pine forest type group consists of the eastern redcedar/hardwood and shortleaf pine forest types. In tables 3 and 6 and fig. 2, the maple/beech/birch forest type group in Kansas is primarily made up of elm/ash/locust; pinyon/juniper is entirely eastern redcedar; and oak/pine is mainly redcedar/hardwood.
[2]See footnote 2 on page 2.

Volume

The net volume of all live trees on forest land, which includes growing stock, rough trees, and rotten trees, was 2.75 billion cubic feet (table 4). Hardwoods constituted just under 2.7 billion cubic feet, and softwoods were more than 92 million cubic feet of all live tree volume. Net volume of all oaks was 498 million cubic feet or 18.8 percent of all hardwood live tree volume. Select oaks (red and white) constituted 372 million cubic feet in volume or 74.8 percent of all oaks and 14.0 percent of all hardwood live tree volume.

On timberland, net volume of all live trees and salvable dead trees was 2.73 billion cubic feet (table 5, fig. 4). Net volume of all live trees was 2.69 billion cubic feet or 98.4 percent of total live tree volume. The difference between the total volume of all live trees on timberland and the total volume of all live trees on forest land (2.75 billion cubic feet) (table 4) represents timber on land that is either low productivity (incapable of growth greater than 20 cubic feet per acre per year at the culmination of mean annual increment) or reserved (e.g., parks, wilderness areas). Of the 1.45 billion cubic feet of growing-stock volume, 1.10 billion cubic feet or 76 percent was sawtimber volume.

Hardwoods constituted 97.2 percent of total sawtimber volume and softwoods were 2.8 percent of the total.

Cull[4] tree volume, at 1.2 billion cubic feet, was 46.1 percent of all live trees. The softwood cull tree volume represented 35.9 percent of the total live-tree softwood volume, whereas hardwood culls represented 46.4 percent of the total hardwood volume. The phototropic and decurrent growth habits of hardwoods and the poor stem form resulting from inadequate self-pruning, particularly in more open stands, might explain the disparity in the cull percentage. The large amount of volume growing in low-density stands, particularly those formerly classified as woody pastures, as well as the large number of noncommercial species tallied, would also explain the high total percentage of cull trees.

The net volume of growing stock on timberland totaled 1.45 billion cubic feet (table 6). Growing-stock volume has substantially increased since 1965 (fig. 5). More than 97

---

[4]Classifying a tree as cull follows strict guidelines of projected number of logs and log lengths and tree species. Local utilization standards may permit the utilization of trees classified in this inventory as "cull."

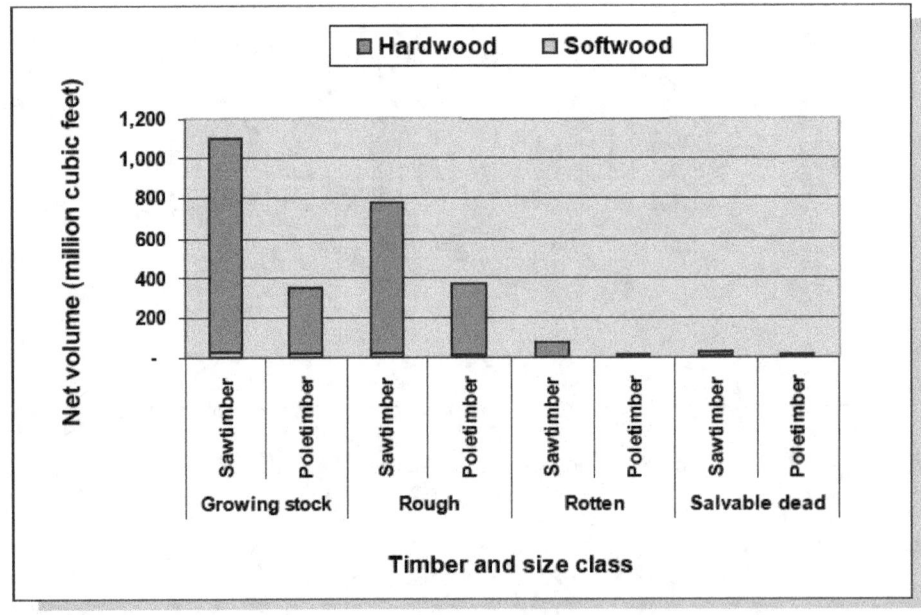

Figure 4. — *Net volume on timberland, in million cubic feet, by timber class and size class, Kansas, 2001-2004.*

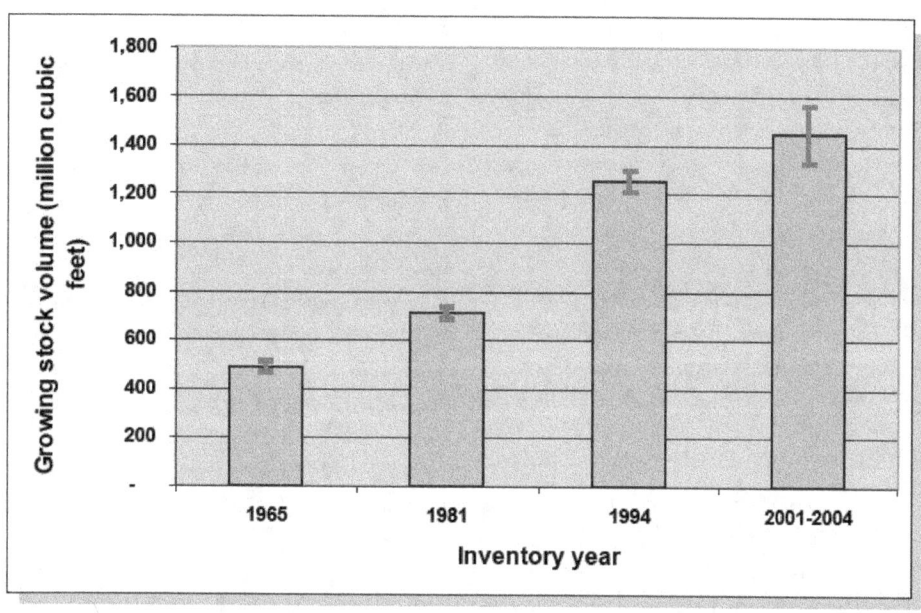

Figure 5. — *Net volume of growing stock on timberland, in millions of cubic feet, for Kansas, 1965-2004.*

percent of that total was in hardwood forest types, 2 percent (29.2 million cubic feet) was in conifer forest types, and the remainder was in the nonstocked category. Table 6 reports the volumes for softwoods and hardwoods for each forest type group. For example, the oak/pine group had 14.0 million cubic feet of softwoods and 19.4 million cubic feet of hardwoods (fig. 6).

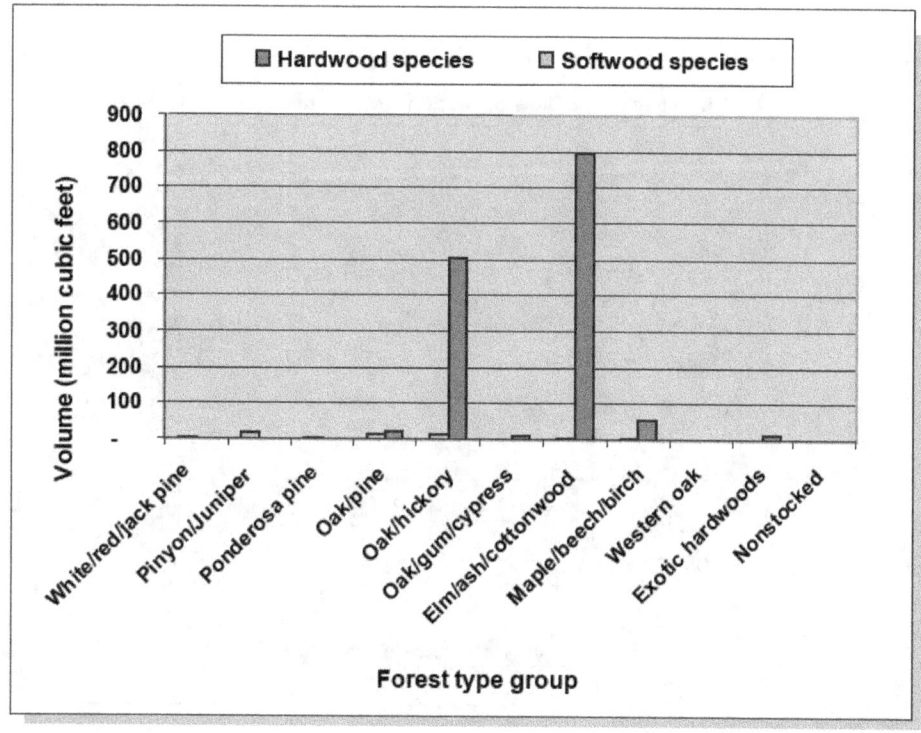

Figure 6. — *Net volume of growing stock on timberland by forest type group, in millions of cubic feet, for Kansas, 2001-2004.*

Table 7 shows net volume of growing stock on timberland by species group and diameter class. The totals for softwood and hardwood volumes, 57.6 million cubic feet and 1.4 billion cubic feet, respectively, are the same as the totals at the bottom of the columns in table 6. Total volume of oak growing stock on timberland was 288.2 million cubic feet, which was 20.7 percent of all hardwood volume and 19.9 percent of all growing-stock volume. Trees at least 19 inches in diameter constituted 39.4 percent of the net volume of hardwood growing stock.

The net volume of sawtimber on timberland was 5.3 billion board feet (table 8). As with many other measures of coverage and abundance in Kansas, hardwoods constituted the preponderance of the volume (97.1 percent or 5.1 billion board feet). Red and white oaks totaled 1.2 billion board feet or 22.6 percent of the hardwood volume. Trees 19 or more inches in diameter were 53 percent of the hardwood volume (2.7 billion board feet). In 1994, the 19+ inch diameter classes constituted 50.8 percent of the total hardwood volume (Leatherberry et al. 1999).

Biomass

The live aboveground biomass on timberland in Kansas totaled 70.6 million dry tons (table 9). More than 5 percent of that total was in 1- to 5-inch trees, 49.4 percent was in growing-stock trees, and 45.4 percent was in non-growing-stock trees. Private landowners held 94.3 percent or 66.6 million tons; public landowners held 5.7 percent (4 million dry tons). Of the 34.9 million dry tons in growing-stock trees, 92.1 percent were on private land and 7.9 percent were on public land. Among non-growing-stock trees, 96.5 percent were on private land and 3.5 percent were on public land (fig. 7).

Close to 73 percent of the total biomass of growing-stock trees was in the boles, and the remaining 26.6 percent was in stumps, tops, and limbs. Approximately the same proportions existed for the 32.1 million dry tons of non-growing-stock trees: 72.5 percent was in bolewood and 27.5 percent was in stumps, tops, and limbs.

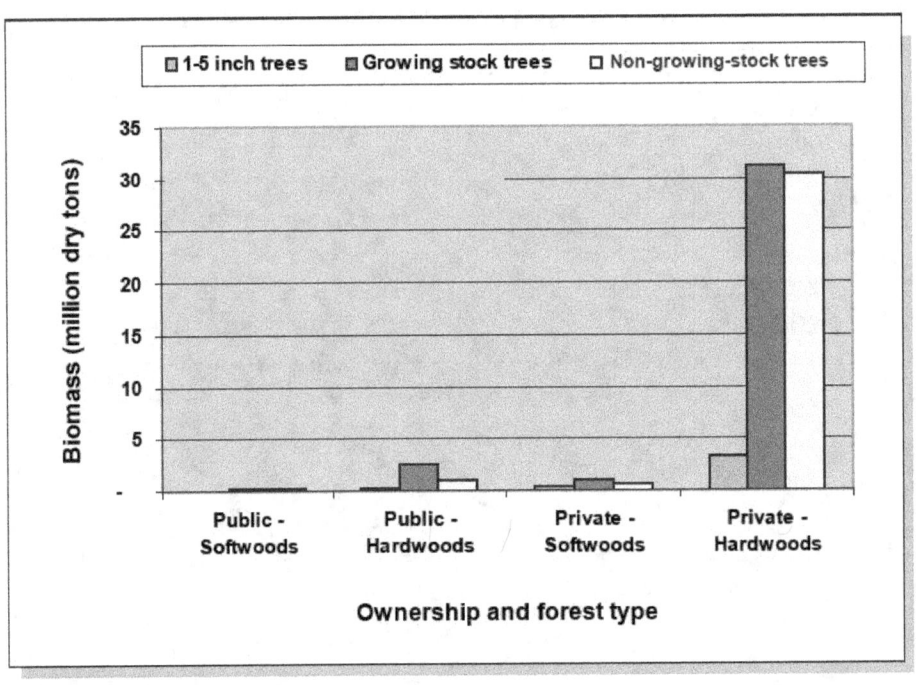

Figure 7. — *Live aboveground biomass in Kansas, 2001-2004, in millions of dry tons, by ownership and forest type.*

An interesting facet of these data is the relatively small proportion of aboveground biomass in non-growing-stock softwood trees (27.8 percent of all softwood biomass) versus non-growing-stock hardwood trees (46.5 percent of all hardwood biomass). These data suggest that a higher proportion of hardwood volume is made up of species of little or no commercial value and that hardwoods are more likely to have defects that result in low quality timber.

Further data related to the three most recent inventories of Kansas (2001, 2002 and 2003) are available at: www.ncrs2.fs.fed.us/4801/fiadb/index.htm.

APPENDIX

Inventory Methods

Since the 1998 inventory of Kansas, several changes have been made in NCFIA inventory methods to improve the quality of the inventory as well as to meet increasing demands for timely forest resource information. The most significant difference between inventories was the change from periodic to annual inventories. Historically, NCFIA periodically inventoried each State on a cycle that averaged about 12 years. However, the need for timely and consistent data across large geographical regions, combined with national legislative mandates, resulted in NCFIA's implementation of an annual inventory system.

With the NCFIA annual inventory system, about one-fifth of all field plots is measured each year. This report includes information from plots measured in 2001, 2002, 2003, and 2004: four-fifths of the plots that will be measured. In 2005, the entire inventory cycle will be completed (all of the plots will have been measured) and NCFIA will report and analyze results as a moving 5-year average (2001-2005). With each additional year of plot measurements, a fifth of the plots will be remeasured and an updated report will be prepared. For example, the 2007 measurement will be used to prepare an updated report based on plots measured in 2003 through 2007. Although there are great advantages with an annual inventory, one difficulty is reporting on results during the first 4 years. For the 2001-2004 annual panels, approximately 80 percent of all field plots have been measured. Sampling error estimates for the 2004 inventory results are area of forest land, 4.72 percent; area of timberland, 4.90 percent; number of growing-stock trees on timberland, 7.56 percent; volume of growing stock on timberland, 9.32 percent; and volume of sawtimber on timberland, 11.41 percent. These sampling error estimates are higher than those for the last periodic inventory completed in 1994 (e.g., 1.59 percent for timberland area and 2.18 percent for growing-stock volume) because of the smaller samples. Thus, caution should be used when drawing conclusions based on this limited data set. As we complete measurement of additional panels, we will have greater confidence in our results due to the increased number of field plots measured.

Other significant changes between our old and new inventory methodologies include new remote sensing technology, new sampling design and plot configuration, and the gathering of additional remotely sensed and field data. Advancements in remote sensing technology since the previous inventory in 1994 have allowed NCFIA to use classifications of Multi-Resolution Land Characterization (MRLC) data and other available remote sensing products to stratify the total area of the State and improve the precision of estimates.

New algorithms were used in 2001-2004 to assign forest type and stand-size class to each condition observed on a plot. These algorithms are being used nationwide by FIA to increase consistency among States and will be used to reassign the forest type and stand-size class of every plot measured in the 1994 inventory when it is updated. This will be done so that changes in forest type and stand-size class will more accurately reflect actual changes in the forest and not changes in how values are computed. The list of recognized forest types, grouping of these forest types for reporting purposes, models used to assign stocking values to individual trees, definition of nonstocked, and names given to the forest types changed with the new algorithms. As a result, comparisons between the published 2001-2004 inventory results and those published for the 1994 inventory may not be valid. For additional details about algorithms used in both inventories, please contact NCFIA.

Inventory Phases

The 2004 Kansas survey was based on a three-phase inventory. The first phase used classified satellite imagery to stratify the state and aerial photographs to select plots for measurement. The second phase measured the traditional FIA suite of mensurational variables, and the third phase focused on a suite of variables related to the health of the forest.

The only land that could not be sampled was (1) private land where field personnel could not obtain permission from the owner to measure the field plot and (2) plots that could not be accessed because of a hazard or danger to field personnel. The methods used in the preparation of this report make the necessary adjustments to account for sites where access was denied or hazardous.

Phase 1

The 2004 inventory used a classification of satellite imagery. FIA used the imagery to form two initial strata—forest and nonforest. Pixels within 60 m (2 pixel widths) of a forest/nonforest boundary formed two additional strata—forest edge and nonforest edge. Forest pixels within 60 m on the forest side of a forest/nonforest boundary were classified into a forest edge stratum. Pixels within 60 m of the boundary on the nonforest side were classified into a nonforest edge stratum. In addition, all strata were divided into public or private ownership based on information available in the Protected Lands Database (DellaSala *et al.* 2001). The estimated population total for a variable is the sum across all strata of the product of each stratum's area (from the pixel count) and the variable's mean per unit area (from plot measurements) for the stratum.

Phase 2

Phase 2 of the inventory consisted of the measurement of 7,094 field plots in Kansas, 385 of which were found to contain forest land. Current FIA precision standards for annual inventories require a sampling intensity of one plot for approximately every 6,000 acres. FIA has divided the entire area of the United States into nonoverlapping hexagons, each of which contains 5,937 acres (McRoberts 1999). An array of field plots was created by establishing one plot within each hexagon (McRoberts 1999). This array of plots is designated the Federal base sample and is considered an equal probability sample; its measurement in Kansas is funded by the Federal government. No additional sample plots beyond the Federal base sample were taken in Kansas.

The total Federal base sample of plots was systematically divided into five interpenetrating, nonoverlapping subsamples or panels. Each year the plots in a single panel are measured, and panels are selected on a 5-year, rotating basis (McRoberts 1999). For estimation purposes, the measurement of each panel of plots may be considered an independent systematic sample of all land in a State. Field crews measure vegetation on plots currently classified as forest by trained photointerpreters using aerial photos or digital orthoquads.

Phase 3

NCFIA has two categories of field plot measurements—phase 2 field plots (standard FIA plots) and phase 3 plots (forest health plots)—to optimize our ability to collect data when available for measurement. Both types of plots are systematically distributed both geographically and temporally. Phase 3 plots are measured with the full suite of forest health monitoring vegetative and health variables (Mangold 1998) collected as well as the full suite of measures associated with phase 2 plots. Phase 3 plots must be measured between June 1 and August 30 to accommodate the additional measurement of nonwoody understory vegetation, ground cover, soils, and other variables. The 2001-2004 annual inventory results represent field measures on 385 phase 2 forested plots and 29 phase 3 field plots.

The new national FIA plot configuration (fig. 8) was first used for data collection in Kansas in 2001, the first annual inventory year. This configuration will be used in subsequent years. The national plot configuration requires mapping forest conditions on each plot.

The estimation of change factors such as growth, mortality, and removals requires data from the remeasurement of plots, two measurements of the same plot taken several years apart. Because of the change to the national plot configuration, NCFIA will not have remeasurement information until the 2006 measurements. Until plot remeasurement data are available, we will be able to report

estimates of only the current state of the forest. The 2006 panel measurements will provide change observations on only one-fifth of our sample plots. Consequently, we will not report change estimates in Kansas until at least four annual panels have been remeasured in 2009. When the annual inventory has been completed in 2010, the full range of change data will be available.

The overall plot layout for the new configuration consists of four subplots. The centers of subplots 2, 3, and 4 are located 120 feet from the center of subplot 1. The azimuths to subplots 2, 3, and 4 are 0, 120, and 240 degrees, respectively. The center of the new plot is located at the same point as the center of the previous plot if a previous plot existed within the sample unit. Trees with a d.b.h. 5 inches and larger are measured on a 24-foot-radius (1/24 acre) circular subplot. All trees less than 5 inches d.b.h. are measured on a 6.8-foot-radius (1/300 acre) circular microplot located 12 feet east of the center of each of the four subplots. Forest conditions that occur on any of the four subplots are recorded. Factors that differentiate forest conditions are changes in forest type, stand-size class, land use, ownership, and density. Each condition that occurs anywhere on any of the subplots is identified, described, and mapped if the area of the condition meets or exceeds 1 acre in size.

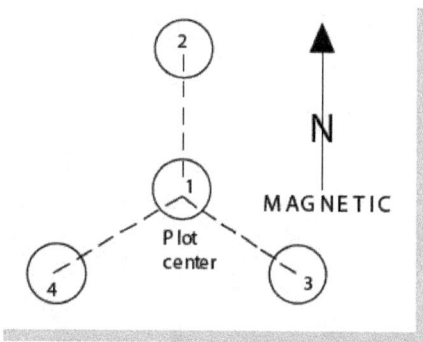

Figure 8. — Current NCFIA field plot design.

Field plot measurements are combined with
phase 1 estimates in the compilation process
and table production. The number of tables
presented here is limited. However, other
tabular data can be generated at: www.ncrs2.
fs.fed.us/4801/fiadb/index.htm.

For additional information, contact:

Program Manager
Forest Inventory and Analysis
North Central Research Station
1992 Folwell Ave.
St. Paul, MN 55108

or

State Forester
Kansas Forest Service
2610 Claflin Road
Manhattan, KS 66502

LITERATURE CITED

Chase, C.D.; Strickler, J.K. 1968.
Kansas woodlands. Resour. Bull. NC-4. St. Paul, MN: U.S. Department of Agriculture, Forest Service, North Central Forest Experiment Station. 50 p.

DellaSala, D.A.; Staus, N.L.; Strittholt, J.R.; et al. 2001.
An updated protected areas database for the United States and Canada. Natural Areas Journal. 21(2): 124-135.

Kansas State College. 1939.
Woodlands of Kansas. Bull. 285. Manhattan, KS: Kansas State College Agricultural Experiment Station. 42 p.

Leatherberry, E.C.; Schmidt, T.L.; Strickler, J.K.; Aslin, R.G. 1999.
An analysis of the forest resources of Kansas. Res. Pap. NC-334. St. Paul, MN: U.S. Department of Agriculture, Forest Service, North Central Research Station. 114 p.

Mangold, R.D. 1998.
Forest health monitoring field methods guide (National 1998). Research Triangle Park, NC: U.S. Department of Agriculture, Forest Service, National Forest Health Monitoring Program. 429 p. (Revision 0, April 1998)

McRoberts, R.E. 1999.
Joint annual forest inventory and monitoring system, the North Central perspective. Journal of Forestry. 97(12): 27-31.

Raile, G.K.; Spencer, J.S. 1984.
Kansas forest statistics, 1981. Resour. Bull. NC-70. St. Paul, MN: U.S. Department of Agriculture, Forest Service, North Central Forest Experiment Station. 124 p.

Spencer, J.S.; Strickler, J.K.; Moyer, W.J. 1984.
Kansas forest inventory, 1981. Resour. Bull. NC-83. St. Paul, MN: U.S. Department of Agriculture, Forest Service, North Central Forest Experiment Station. 134 p.

TABLE TITLES

Table 1.—*Area of forest land by forest type group, forest type, and owner category, Kansas, 2001-2004*

Table 2.—*Area of timberland by major forest type group, stand origin, and owner category, Kansas, 2001-2004*

Table 3.—*Area of timberland by forest type group, forest type, and stand-size class, Kansas, 2001-2004*

Table 4.—*Net volume of all live trees on forest land by species group, species, and owner category, Kansas, 2001-2004*

Table 5.—*Net volume of all live trees and salvable dead trees on timberland by class of timber and softwood/hardwood species category, Kansas, 2001-2004*

Table 6.—*Net volume of growing stock on timberland by forest type group, forest type, and softwood/hardwood species category, Kansas, 2001-2004*

Table 7.—*Net volume of growing stock on timberland by species group, species, and diameter class, Kansas, 2001-2004*

Table 8.—*Net volume of sawtimber on timberland by species group, species, and diameter class, Kansas, 2001-2004*

Table 9.—*All live aboveground tree biomass on timberland by owner category, softwood/hardwood species category, and tree biomass component, Kansas, 2001-2004*

TABLES

Table 1. -- Area of forest land by forest type group, forest type, and owner category, Kansas, 2001-2004

(In thousand acres)

Forest type group/ forest type	All owners	Owner category		
		Public	Private	Unidentified owner
Softwood type groups				
White / red / jack pine group				
Red pine	3.9	3.9	- -	- -
All forest types	3.9	3.9	- -	- -
Pinyon / juniper group				
Eastern redcedar	103.9	1.7	102.2	- -
All forest types	103.9	1.7	102.2	- -
Ponderosa pine group				
Ponderosa pine	8.9	8.9	- -	- -
All forest types	8.9	8.9	- -	- -
All softwood groups	116.6	14.4	102.2	- -
Hardwood type groups				
Oak / pine group				
Eastern redcedar / hardwood	70.8	- -	70.8	- -
All forest types	70.8	- -	70.8	- -
Oak / hickory group				
Post oak / blackjack oak	129.2	4.8	124.4	- -
White oak / red oak / hickory	250.1	16.9	233.1	- -
Northern red oak	8.8	- -	8.8	- -
Sassafras / persimmon	5.0	- -	5.0	- -
Bur oak	48.4	- -	48.4	- -
Black walnut	36.8	- -	36.8	- -
Mixed upland hardwoods	632.8	20.6	612.2	- -
All forest types	1,111.0	42.3	1,068.8	- -
Oak / gum / cypress group				
Swamp chestnut oak / cherrybark oak	6.8	- -	6.8	- -
All forest types	6.8	- -	6.8	- -

(Table 1 continued on next page)

(Table 1 continued)

Forest type group/ forest type	Owner category			
	All owners	Public	Private	Unidentified owner
Hardwood type groups				
Elm / ash / cottonwood group				
Elm / ash / cottonwood group	1.9	--	1.9	--
Black ash / American elm / red maple	0.8	--	0.8	--
River birch / sycamore	37.2	--	37.2	--
Cottonwood	104.7	25.3	79.5	--
Willow	16.0	3.6	12.4	--
Sycamore / pecan / American elm	40.7	--	40.7	--
Sugarberry / hackberry / elm / green ash	386.6	19.3	367.3	--
Silver maple / American elm	14.4	--	14.4	--
Cottonwood / willow	28.1	--	28.1	--
All forest types	630.3	48.1	582.2	--
Maple / beech / birch group				
Sugar maple / beech / yellow birch	40.4	--	40.4	--
Elm / ash / locust	89.3	5.4	83.8	--
All forest types	129.7	5.4	124.3	--
Western oak group				
Deciduous oak woodland	1.6	--	1.6	--
All forest types	1.6	--	1.6	--
Exotic hardwoods group				
Other exotic hardwoods	34.7	1.9	32.9	--
All forest types	34.7	1.9	32.9	--
All hardwood groups	1,985.0	97.7	1,887.3	--
Nonstocked	24.5	--	24.5	--
All forest groups	2,126.1	112.1	2,014.0	--

All table cells without observations in the inventory sample are indicated by --. Table value of 0.0 indicates the acres round to less than 0.1 thousand acres. Columns and rows may not add to their totals due to rounding.

Table 2. -- Area of timberland by major forest type group, stand origin, and owner category, Kansas, 2001-2004

(In thousand acres)

Major forest type group and stand origin	All owners	Owner category		
		Public	Private	Unidentified owner
Softwood type groups				
Natural	89.3	--	89.3	--
Planted	20.9	12.7	8.2	--
All softwood types	110.1	12.7	97.4	--
Hardwood type groups				
Natural	1,886.1	95.8	1,790.3	--
Planted	28.3	--	28.3	--
All hardwood types	1,914.4	95.8	1,818.6	--
Nonstocked	24.5	--	24.5	--
All groups	2,049.0	108.5	1,940.5	--

All table cells without observations in the inventory sample are indicated by --. Table value of 0.0 indicates the acres round to less than 0.1 thousand acres. Columns and rows may not add to their totals due to rounding.

16

Table 3. — Area of timberland by forest type group, forest type, and
stand-size class, Kansas, 2001-2004

(In thousand acres)

Forest type group/ forest type	All stands	Sawtimber	Poletimber	Sapling-seedling	Non-stocked
Softwood type groups					
White / red / jack pine group					
Red pine	3.9	3.9	- -	- -	- -
All forest types	3.9	3.9	- -	- -	- -
Pinyon / juniper group					
Eastern redcedar	97.4	8.2	38.3	50.9	- -
All forest types	97.4	8.2	38.3	50.9	- -
Ponderosa pine group					
Ponderosa pine	8.9	- -	8.9	- -	- -
All forest types	8.9	- -	8.9	- -	- -
All softwood groups	110.1	12.0	47.2	50.9	- -
Hardwood type groups					
Oak / pine group					
Eastern redcedar / hardwood	65.9	28.1	19.6	18.2	- -
All forest types	65.9	28.1	19.6	18.2	- -
Oak / hickory group					
Post oak / blackjack oak	100.3	23.6	56.5	20.2	- -
White oak / red oak / hickory	248.2	115.3	83.1	49.9	- -
Northern red oak	8.8	8.8	- -	- -	- -
Sassafras / persimmon	5.0	5.0	- -	- -	- -
Bur oak	48.4	48.0	0.4	- -	- -
Black walnut	36.8	23.6	10.8	2.4	- -
Mixed upland hardwoods	613.9	162.6	337.9	113.4	- -
All forest types	1,061.5	386.9	488.7	185.9	- -
Oak / gum / cypress group					
Swamp chestnut oak / cherrybark oak	6.8	- -	6.8	- -	- -
All forest types	6.8	- -	6.8	- -	- -

(Table 3 continued on next page)

(Table 3 continued)

	Stand-size class				
Forest type group/ forest type	All stands	Sawtimber	Poletimber	Sapling-seedling	Non-stocked
Hardwood type groups					
Elm / ash / cottonwood group					
Elm / ash / cottonwood group	1.9	- -	1.9	- -	- -
Black ash / American elm / red maple	0.8	- -	0.8	- -	- -
River birch / sycamore	37.2	29.9	5.6	1.7	- -
Cottonwood	102.7	102.7	- -	- -	- -
Willow	16.0	- -	- -	16.0	- -
Sycamore / pecan / American elm	40.7	21.6	17.4	1.7	- -
Sugarberry / hackberry / elm / green ash	381.5	268.9	73.7	38.9	- -
Silver maple / American elm	14.4	7.8	- -	6.6	- -
Cottonwood / willow	28.1	23.3	4.8	- -	- -
All forest types	623.3	454.3	104.2	64.8	- -
Maple / beech / birch group					
Sugar maple / beech / yellow birch	40.4	19.8	20.6	- -	- -
Elm / ash / locust	82.0	43.7	31.5	6.8	- -
All forest types	122.4	63.5	52.1	6.8	- -
Western oak group					
Deciduous oak woodland	1.6	- -	1.6	- -	- -
All forest types	1.6	- -	1.6	- -	- -
Exotic hardwoods group					
Other exotic hardwoods	32.9	9.5	15.4	7.9	- -
All forest types	32.9	9.5	15.4	7.9	- -
All hardwood groups	1,914.4	942.4	688.4	283.6	- -
Nonstocked	24.5	- -	- -	- -	24.5
All forest groups	2,049.0	954.5	735.6	334.5	24.5

All table cells without observations in the inventory sample are indicated by --. Table value of 0.0 indicates the acres round to less than 0.1 thousand acres. Columns and rows may not add to their totals due to rounding.

Table 4. – Net volume of all live trees on forest land by species group, species, and owner category, Kansas, 2001-2004

(In thousand cubic feet)

Species group/ species	Owner category			
	All owners	Public	Private	Unidentified owner
Softwoods				
Loblolly and shortleaf pines				
Shortleaf pine	2,158	2,158	- -	- -
All species	2,158	2,158	- -	- -
Eastern white and red pines				
Red pine	3,637	3,637	- -	- -
Eastern white pine	2,039	2,039	- -	- -
All species	5,675	5,675	- -	- -
Other eastern softwoods				
Eastern redcedar	76,529	3,539	72,990	- -
Ponderosa pine	7,740	4,644	3,096	- -
All species	84,269	8,183	76,086	- -
Total softwoods	92,103	16,017	76,086	- -
Hardwoods				
Select white oaks				
White oak	6,930	- -	6,930	- -
Bur oak	161,222	3,504	157,719	- -
Chinkapin oak	103,725	8,338	95,387	- -
All species	271,877	11,841	260,036	- -
Select red oaks				
Northern red oak	93,385	6,110	87,276	- -
Shumard oak	7,127	- -	7,127	- -
All species	100,513	6,110	94,403	- -
Other white oaks				
Overcup oak	139	- -	139	- -
Post oak	64,881	5,639	59,243	- -
All species	65,020	5,639	59,382	- -
Other red oaks				
Shingle oak	4,656	4,656	- -	- -
Blackjack oak	18,043	26	18,016	- -
Pin oak	25,966	243	25,723	- -
Black oak	11,798	56	11,743	- -
All species	60,463	4,981	55,481	- -

(Table 4 continued on next page)

(Table 4 continued)

Species group/ species	All owners	Owner category		
		Public	Private	Unidentified owner
Hardwoods				
Hickory				
Bitternut hickory	30,733	367	30,366	--
Pecan	26,485	88	26,397	--
Shellbark hickory	2,762	--	2,762	--
Shagbark hickory	24,041	2,832	21,209	--
Black hickory	3,381	--	3,381	--
Mockernut hickory	2,161	--	2,161	--
All species	89,563	3,287	86,276	--
Hard maple				
Sugar maple	11,353	1,398	9,954	--
All species	11,353	1,398	9,954	--
Soft maple				
Red maple	54	--	54	--
Silver maple	47,166	11,791	35,375	--
All species	47,220	11,791	35,429	--
Ash				
White ash	21,001	--	21,001	--
Green ash	221,510	10,469	211,041	--
Blue ash	210	--	210	--
All species	242,721	10,469	232,253	--
Cottonwood and aspen				
Eastern cottonwood	278,548	58,470	220,078	--
Plains cottonwood	48,917	--	48,917	--
All species	327,465	58,470	268,995	--
Basswood				
American basswood	5,739	--	5,739	--
All species	5,739	--	5,739	--
Black walnut				
Black walnut	175,968	2,637	173,331	--
All species	175,968	2,637	173,331	--

(Table 4 continued on next page)

(Table 4 continued)

Species group/species	Owner category			
	All owners	Public	Private	Unidentified owner
Hardwoods				
Other eastern soft hardwoods				
Boxelder	41,580	2,187	39,393	--
Texas buckeye	1,092	--	1,092	--
Northern catalpa	24,310	--	24,310	--
Sugarberry	2,970	--	2,970	--
Hackberry	330,924	8,080	322,843	--
American sycamore	87,752	3,467	84,285	--
Black cherry	5,695	--	5,695	--
Black willow	44,554	2,040	42,514	--
White willow	137	--	137	--
American elm	219,448	7,655	211,793	--
Siberian elm	44,773	1,218	43,555	--
Slippery elm	14,896	39	14,857	--
All species	818,132	24,687	793,445	--
Other eastern hard hardwoods				
Common persimmon	1,670	--	1,670	--
Honeylocust	97,644	1,369	96,275	--
Kentucky coffeetree	14,563	710	13,853	--
Mulberry spp.	5,171	4,674	497	--
White mu berry	86	--	86	--
Red mu berry	120,992	5,308	115,685	--
Black locust	9,785	--	9,785	--
Rock elm	190	--	190	--
All species	250,101	12,060	238,041	--

(Table 4 continued on next page)

(Table 4 continued)

Hardwoods

Species group/ species	Owner category			
	All owners	Public	Private	Unidentified owner
Eastern noncommercial hardwoods				
Ailanthus	328	--	328	--
Serviceberry spp.		--		--
Pawpaw		--		--
Chittamwood, gum bumelia	515	--	515	--
American hornbeam, musclewood	249	--	249	--
Southern catalpa	1,495	--	1,495	--
Eastern redbud	6,494	302	6,192	--
Hawthorn spp.		--		--
Downy hawthorn		--		--
Osage-orange	167,259	4,684	162,574	--
Eastern hophornbeam	803	--	803	--
Cherry and plum spp.	145	--	145	--
American plum	377	--	377	--
Western soapberry	1,330	--	1,330	--
Peachleaf willow	8,472	--	8,472	--
Russian-olive	216	--	216	--
All species	187,683	4,986	182,697	--
Total hardwoods	2,653,818	158,356	2,495,463	--
All species groups	2,745,922	174,373	2,571,549	--

All table cells without observations in the inventory sample are indicated by --. Table value of 0 indicates the volume rounds to less than 1 thousand cubic feet. Columns and rows may not add to their totals due to rounding.

22

Table 5. -- Net volume of all live trees and salvable dead trees on timberland
by class of timber and softwood/hardwood species category, Kansas, 2001-2004

(In thousand cubic feet)

Class of timber	All species	Softwood species	Hardwood species
Live trees			
Growing-stock trees			
Sawtimber			
Saw log portion	983,200	27,206	955,994
Upper stem portion	118,908	3,799	115,109
Total	1,102,108	31,005	1,071,103
Poletimber	348,202	26,580	321,622
All growing-stock trees	1,450,311	57,585	1,392,725
Cull trees			
Rough trees[1]			
Sawtimber size	781,037	20,502	760,535
Poletimber size	366,149	11,818	354,331
Total	1,147,186	32,320	1,114,866
Rotten trees[1]			
Sawtimber size	77,400	- -	77,400
Poletimber size	14,091	- -	14,091
Total	91,491	- -	91,491
All live cull trees	1,238,677	32,320	1,206,357
All live trees	2,688,987	89,905	2,599,082
Salvable dead trees			
Sawtimber size	30,839	3,914	26,925
Poletimber size	11,645	700	10,944
All salvable dead trees	42,483	4,614	37,869
All classes	2,731,471	94,519	2,636,952

All table cells without observations in the inventory sample are indicated by --. Table value of 0 indicates
the volume rounds to less than 1 thousand cubic feet. Columns and rows may not add to their totals due
to rounding.
[1] Includes noncommercial species.

Table 6. -- Net volume of growing stock on timberland by forest type group,
forest type, and softwood/hardwood species category, Kansas, 2001-2004

(In thousand cubic feet)

Forest type group/ forest type	All species	Softwood species	Hardwood species
Softwood type groups			
White / red / jack pine group			
Red pine	5,017	5,017	- -
All forest types	5,017	5,017	- -
Pinyon / juniper group			
Eastern redcedar	20,666	18,690	1,976
All forest types	20,666	18,690	1,976
Ponderosa pine group			
Ponderosa pine	3,520	3,355	165
All forest types	3,520	3,355	165
All softwood groups	29,203	27,063	2,141
Hardwood type groups			
Oak / pine group			
Eastern redcedar / hardwood	33,384	13,959	19,426
All forest types	33,384	13,959	19,426
Oak / hickory group			
Post oak / blackjack oak	51,184	642	50,543
White oak / red oak / hickory	204,681	1,252	203,429
Northern red oak	21,619	- -	21,619
Sassafras / persimmon	5,616	- -	5,616
Bur oak	36,508	1,549	34,959
Black walnut	21,059	128	20,930
Mixed upland hardwoods	172,523	7,671	164,853
All forest types	513,190	11,241	501,949
Oak / gum / cypress group			
Swamp chestnut oak / cherrybark oak	6,739	89	6,650
All forest types	6,739	89	6,650

(Table 6 continued on next page)

24

(Table 6 continued)

Forest type group/ forest type	All species	Softwood species	Hardwood species
Hardwood type groups			
Elm / ash / cottonwood group			
Elm / ash / cottonwood group	195	--	195
Black ash / American elm / red maple	702	111	590
River birch / sycamore	57,416	--	57,416
Cottonwood	242,397	1,052	241,344
Willow	2,580	--	2,580
Sycamore / pecan / American elm	67,724	--	67,724
Sugarberry / hackberry / elm / green ash	373,265	1,474	371,791
Silver maple / American elm	21,956	--	21,956
Cottonwood / willow	31,155	--	31,155
All forest types	797,389	2,638	794,751
Maple / beech / birch group			
Sugar maple / beech / yellow birch	27,368	797	26,571
Elm / ash / locust	29,886	1,560	28,326
All forest types	57,254	2,357	54,897
Western oak group			
Deciduous oak woodland	286	--	286
All forest types	286	--	286
Exotic hardwoods group			
Other exotic hardwoods	11,076	67	11,010
All forest types	11,076	67	11,010
All hardwood groups	1,419,318	30,351	1,388,968
Nonstocked	1,789	172	1,617
All forest groups	1,450,311	57,585	1,392,725

All table cells without observations in the inventory sample are indicated by --. Table value of 0 indicates the volume rounds to less than 1 thousand cubic feet. Columns and rows may not add to their totals due to rounding.

Table 7. – Net volume of growing stock on timberland by species group, species, and diameter class, Kansas, 2001-2004

(In thousand cubic feet)

Species group/ species	All classes	Diameter class (inches at breast height)									
		5.0-6.9	7.0-8.9	9.0-10.9	11.0-12.9	13.0-14.9	15.0-16.9	17.0-18.9	19.0-20.9	21.0-28.9	29.0+
Softwoods											
Loblolly and shortleaf pines											
Shortleaf pine	1,890	187	817	885	--	--	--	--	--	--	--
All species	1,890	187	817	885	--	--	--	--	--	--	--
Eastern white and red pines											
Red pine	2,490	--	--	--	--	905	1,585	--	--	--	--
Eastern white pine	638	--	--	--	638	--	--	--	--	--	--
All species	3,127	--	--	--	638	905	1,585	--	--	--	--
Other eastern softwoods											
Eastern redcedar	48,028	12,701	11,515	8,272	8,772	4,553	2,216	--	--	--	--
Ponderosa pine	4,540	--	1,360	--	637	1,197	1,346	--	--	--	--
All species	52,568	12,701	12,875	8,272	9,409	5,750	3,562	--	--	--	--
Total softwoods	57,585	12,888	13,692	9,157	10,046	6,655	5,147	--	--	--	--
Hardwoods											
Select white oaks											
Bur oak	79,841	1,224	2,132	4,275	7,897	2,459	7,044	3,430	8,708	35,863	6,809
Chinkapin oak	53,592	1,401	2,961	5,140	4,076	5,034	1,117	7,281	2,596	23,985	--
All species	133,432	2,625	5,093	9,415	11,973	7,493	8,160	10,711	11,304	59,849	6,809
Select red oaks											
Northern red oak	78,339	3,037	2,381	2,600	1,595	5,967	6,804	7,659	9,520	32,111	6,666
Shumard oak	7,015	--	349	325	664	2,766	1,175	1,736	--	--	--
All species	85,354	3,037	2,730	2,924	2,259	8,734	7,979	9,395	9,520	32,111	6,666
Other white oaks											
Overcup oak	139	--	139	--	--	--	--	--	--	--	--
Post oak	32,421	6,399	8,007	10,559	3,749	1,958	--	--	1,750	--	--
All species	32,560	6,399	8,146	10,559	3,749	1,958	--	--	1,750	--	--
Other red oaks											
Shingle oak	1,537	--	--	--	--	--	--	1,537	--	--	--
Blackjack oak	1,876	204	878	--	793	--	--	--	--	--	--
Pin oak	24,254	789	1,809	1,979	1,301	1,040	--	--	1,939	4,742	10,655
Black oak	9,208	262	611	321	1,424	1,148	3,818	1,625	--	--	--
All species	36,875	1,256	3,298	2,299	3,518	2,188	3,818	3,162	1,939	4,742	10,655
Hickory											
Bitternut hickory	25,834	3,517	3,803	4,289	2,326	6,109	3,921	1,869	--	--	--
Pecan	11,962	765	1,393	1,746	5,045	--	--	--	--	3,013	--
Shellbark hickory	2,762	350	889	--	--	1,522	--	--	--	--	--
Shagbark hickory	20,524	4,021	6,110	3,531	3,925	2,937	--	--	--	--	--
Black hickory	882	--	--	--	882	--	--	--	--	--	--
Mockernut hickory	1,375	65	--	--	--	--	1,309	--	--	--	--
All species	63,339	8,719	12,195	9,566	12,178	10,568	5,230	1,869	--	3,013	--
Hard maple											
Sugar maple	6,788	378	1,840	1,835	--	2,735	--	--	--	--	--
All species	6,788	378	1,840	1,835	--	2,735	--	--	--	--	--

(Table 7 continued on next page)

26

(Table 7 continued)

Species group/species	All classes	Diameter class (inches at breast height)									
		5.0-6.9	7.0-8.9	9.0-10.9	11.0-12.9	13.0-14.9	15.0-16.9	17.0-18.9	19.0-20.9	21.0-28.9	29.0+
Hardwoods											
Soft maple											
Silver maple	38,324	875	1,035	1,787	--	3,436	4,147	4,786	9,325	3,128	9,804
All species	38,324	875	1,035	1,787	--	3,436	4,147	4,786	9,325	3,128	9,804
Ash											
White ash	16,990	2,839	1,228	1,815	3,252	1,016	--	2,894	--	3,946	--
Green ash	131,424	6,748	11,965	17,465	16,360	24,502	13,725	15,774	12,746	12,139	--
Blue ash	210	--	210	--	--	--	--	--	--	--	--
All species	148,624	9,587	13,404	19,280	19,612	25,518	13,725	18,668	12,746	16,085	--
Cottonwood and aspen											
Eastern cottonwood	188,754	467	1,303	3,081	3,247	8,552	6,461	14,134	13,326	46,244	91,939
Plains cottonwood	44,508	--	247	545	3,692	2,256	10,968	4,087	5,154	17,558	--
All species	233,262	467	1,550	3,626	6,939	10,808	17,429	18,221	18,480	63,802	91,939
Basswood											
American basswood	1,361	138	437	--	786	--	--	--	--	--	--
All species	1,361	138	437	--	786	--	--	--	--	--	--
Black walnut											
Black walnut	115,294	5,927	8,897	13,950	11,546	25,885	17,821	10,250	21,019	--	--
All species	115,294	5,927	8,897	13,950	11,546	25,885	17,821	10,250	21,019	--	--
Other eastern soft hardwoods											
Boxelder	15,456	248	599	1,535	1,600	890	--	4,983	--	--	5,601
Texas buckeye	--	--	--	--	--	--	--	--	--	--	--
Northern catalpa	13,165	--	172	1,256	4,371	769	1,327	5,269	--	--	--
Hackberry	222,237	14,793	23,870	22,967	23,024	30,153	37,354	17,556	15,700	36,820	--
American sycamore	76,202	520	413	1,325	--	2,569	8,314	--	--	28,252	34,809
Black cherry	803	288	--	--	515	--	--	--	--	--	--
Black willow	24,037	536	914	1,299	3,237	4,714	1,402	3,930	2,422	5,584	--
American elm	70,344	11,865	14,116	11,620	4,800	5,766	6,920	5,610	--	4,226	5,421
Siberian elm	9,219	1,391	2,394	2,381	1,070	--	--	1,983	--	--	--
Slippery elm	5,826	1,666	1,242	658	667	--	--	1,592	--	--	--
All species	437,288	31,307	43,719	43,041	39,285	44,861	55,317	40,923	18,122	74,882	45,831
Other eastern hard hardwoods											
Common persimmon	956	461	495	--	--	--	--	--	--	--	--
Honeylocust	25,762	5,015	3,877	3,763	3,830	833	2,306	--	3,674	2,465	--
Kentucky coffeetree	10,860	514	1,204	1,324	1,297	2,005	1,227	--	3,289	--	--
Mulberry spp.	1,583	418	207	--	958	--	--	--	--	--	--
Red mulberry	16,792	928	3,426	4,378	571	--	2,376	--	2,280	2,832	--
Black locust	4,080	783	1,855	1,443	--	--	--	--	--	--	--
Rock elm	190	--	190	--	--	--	--	--	--	--	--
All species	60,224	8,119	11,254	10,908	6,655	2,838	5,909	--	9,243	5,297	--
Total hardwoods	1,392,725	78,833	113,599	129,190	118,498	147,022	139,536	117,986	113,448	262,909	171,705
All species groups	1,450,311	91,721	127,291	138,347	128,544	153,676	144,682	117,986	113,448	262,909	171,705

All table cells without observations in the inventory sample are indicated by --. Table value of 0 indicates the volume rounds to less than 1 thousand cubic feet. Columns and rows may not add to their totals due to rounding.

Table 8. -- Net volume of sawtimber on timberland by species group, species, and diameter class. Kansas, 2001-2004

(In thousand board feet)[1]

Species group/ species	All classes	Diameter class (inches at breast height)							
		9.0-10.9	11.0-12.9	13.0-14.9	15.0-16.9	17.0-18.9	19.0-20.9	21.0-28.9	29.0+
Softwoods									
Loblolly and shortleaf pines									
Shortleaf pine	3,950	3,950	--	--	--	--	--	--	--
All species	3,950	3,950	--	--	--	--	--	--	--
Eastern white and red pines									
Red pine	11,285	--	--	4,003	7,282	--	--	--	--
Eastern white pine	2,757	--	2,757	--	--	--	--	--	--
All species	14,042	--	2,757	4,003	7,282	--	--	--	--
Other eastern softwoods									
Eastern redcedar	122,230	44,832	44,734	22,244	10,420	--	--	--	--
Ponderosa pine	15,309	--	3,040	5,507	6,762	--	--	--	--
All species	137,538	44,832	47,775	27,751	17,181	--	--	--	--
Total softwoods	155,531	48,782	50,532	31,754	24,463	--	--	--	--
Hardwoods									
Select white oaks									
Bur oak	363,298	--	37,560	11,803	34,430	16,950	43,006	182,730	36,820
Chinkapin oak	220,660	--	19,554	24,365	5,368	36,085	12,778	122,509	--
All species	583,958	--	57,114	36,168	39,797	53,035	55,784	305,239	36,820
Select red oaks									
Northern red oak	359,571	--	7,425	28,912	33,506	38,424	48,716	167,478	35,110
Shumard oak	30,874	--	3,125	13,222	5,769	8,757	--	--	--
All species	390,445	--	10,550	42,135	39,275	47,181	48,716	167,478	35,110
Other white oaks									
Post oak	34,712	--	17,122	9,162	--	--	8,429	--	--
All species	34,712	--	17,122	9,162	--	--	8,429	--	--
Other red oaks									
Shingle oak	7,413	--	--	--	--	7,413	--	--	--
Blackjack oak	3,670	--	3,670	--	--	--	--	--	--
Pin oak	100,714	--	5,815	4,941	--	--	9,598	24,633	55,727
Black oak	38,050	--	6,567	5,416	18,194	7,873	--	--	--
All species	149,848	--	16,052	10,357	18,194	15,286	9,598	24,633	55,727
Hickory									
Bitternut hickory	70,332	--	11,163	29,977	19,698	9,494	--	--	--
Pecan	39,849	--	23,521	--	--	--	--	16,328	--
Shellbark hickory	7,331	--	--	7,331	--	--	--	--	--
Shagbark hickory	32,549	--	18,408	14,141	--	--	--	--	--
Black hickory	4,170	--	4,170	--	--	--	--	--	--
Mockernut hickory	6,329	--	--	--	6,329	--	--	--	--
All species	160,559	--	57,262	51,449	26,027	9,494	--	16,328	--
Hard maple									
Sugar maple	13,401	--	--	13,401	--	--	--	--	--
All species	13,401	--	--	13,401	--	--	--	--	--

(Table 8 continued on next page)

(Table 8 continued)

Species group/ species	All classes	Diameter class (inches at breast height)							
		9.0-10.9	11.0-12.9	13.0-14.9	15.0-16.9	17.0-18.9	19.0-20.9	21.0-28.9	29.0+
Hardwoods									
Soft maple									
Silver maple	162,880	--	--	14,784	18,449	21,903	43,389	14,833	49,523
All species	162,880	--	--	14,784	18,449	21,903	43,389	14,833	49,523
Ash									
White ash	50,976	--	13,415	4,386	--	13,412	--	19,763	--
Green ash	435,015	--	68,481	106,874	62,698	74,185	62,011	60,767	--
All species	485,991	--	81,896	111,260	62,698	87,597	62,011	80,530	--
Cottonwood and aspen									
Eastern cottonwood	889,228	--	14,442	38,787	30,681	71,017	67,154	250,094	417,054
Plains cottonwood	207,720	--	15,842	10,165	50,397	18,956	24,493	87,868	--
All species	1,096,948	--	30,284	48,952	81,078	89,973	91,647	337,961	417,054
Basswood									
American basswood	4,038	--	4,038	--	--	--	--	--	--
All species	4,038	--	4,038	--	--	--	--	--	--
Black walnut									
Black walnut	405,536	--	51,015	118,857	84,346	49,187	102,131	--	--
All species	405,536	--	51,015	118,857	84,346	49,187	102,131	--	--
Other eastern soft hardwoods									
Boxelder	58,972	--	6,503	3,709	--	22,063	--	--	26,697
Northern catalpa	51,103	--	18,369	3,267	5,840	23,626	--	--	--
Hackberry	750,731	--	104,119	138,734	174,483	80,885	74,950	177,561	--
American sycamore	379,820	--	--	11,501	39,091	--	--	146,467	182,761
Black cherry	2,064	--	2,064	--	--	--	--	--	--
Black willow	93,111	--	12,679	19,162	6,243	17,200	10,666	27,161	--
American elm	152,397	--	21,801	25,825	32,079	25,538	--	21,140	26,013
Siberian elm	13,630	--	4,639	--	--	8,991	--	--	--
Slippery elm	10,754	--	3,081	--	--	7,673	--	--	--
All species	1,512,581	--	173,255	202,198	257,736	185,977	85,616	372,329	235,470
Other eastern hard hardwoods									
Honeylocust	57,379	--	15,820	3,493	10,064	--	16,595	11,407	--
Kentucky coffeetree	33,818	--	5,313	8,425	5,224	--	14,857	--	--
Mulberry spp.	3,878	--	3,878	--	--	--	--	--	--
Red mulberry	36,173	--	2,384	--	10,535	--	10,412	12,842	--
All species	131,249	--	27,395	11,918	25,823	--	41,863	24,249	--
Total hardwoods	5,132,145	--	525,982	670,639	653,423	559,633	549,184	1,343,580	829,703
All species groups	5,287,676	48,782	576,514	702,393	677,886	559,633	549,184	1,343,580	829,703

All table cells without observations in the inventory sample are indicated by --. Table value of 0 indicates the volume rounds to less than 1 thousand board feet. Columns and rows may not add to their totals due to rounding.
[1] International 1/4-inch rule.

Table 9. -- All live aboveground tree biomass on timberland by owner category, softwood/hardwood species category, and tree biomass component, Kansas, 2001-2004

(In thousand dry tons)

Owner category and softwood/hardwood category	All components	All live 1-5 inch trees	Growing-stock trees			Non-growing-stock trees		
			Total	Boles	Stumps, tops, and limbs	Total	Boles	Stumps, tops, and limbs
Public								
Softwoods	281	6	181	147	34	94	78	16
Hardwoods	3,740	147	2,569	1,926	644	1,023	725	298
Total	4,021	154	2,750	2,072	678	1,117	803	314
Private								
Softwoods	1,919	325	1,014	716	298	580	414	166
Hardwoods	64,655	3,191	31,091	22,778	8,313	30,372	22,034	8,338
Total	66,574	3,516	32,105	23,494	8,611	30,952	22,449	8,504
All ownerships								
Softwoods	2,200	332	1,194	862	332	674	492	181
Hardwoods	68,394	3,338	33,661	24,704	8,957	31,395	22,759	8,636
Total	70,594	3,670	34,855	25,566	9,289	32,069	23,251	8,818

All table cells without observations in the inventory sample are indicated by -- . Table value of 0 indicates the aboveground tree biomass rounds to less than 1 thousand dry ton. Columns and rows may not add to their totals due to rounding.